10 MEDICARE MISTAKES FINANCIAL ADVISORS MAKE AND HOW TO AVOID THEM

Al Kushner

The material contained herein is for informational purposes only, and the opinions and statements are solely those of the author, Al Kushner. The ideas in this book are guidelines, beliefs, and best practices utilized by Mr. Kushner throughout his insurance career. This material should not be construed as an offer to sell or a solicitation to buy any insurance product. Following the guidance contained in this book does not guarantee financial professionals will achieve any level of success in their business.

7 Essential Medicare &
Social Security Forms

File A Medicare Claim

Application For Enrollment in Medicare Part B

Application For Termination of Medicare Part A and or Part B

Enroll in Medicare Easy Pay - Automatic Premium Withdrawal

File A Complaint About The Quality of Healthcare You Received

Income Related Monthly Adjustment (IRMAA) Appeal

Proof of Creditable Coverage When Applying for Medicare

MEDICARE
ENROLLMENT FORM

7 ESSENTIAL MEDICARE & SOCIAL SECURITY FORMS

Download FREE at
MedicareForms.help

TESTIMONIALS

I have worked as a CFP for 20-plus years, and I have to say this is one of the best books I've seen on Medicare. I'm not yet enrolling in Medicare, but I'm not too far off either. The author explains the mistakes not to be made when applying for Medicare benefits—written in a way to make Medicare easily -understandable for the average person. I highly recommend it!

Stephen Z., CFP

This book was recommended by an associate of my company, and I am so happy that I got the book. It was definitely a great recommendation. Not only does Al explain all the Medicare mistakes that advisors make, he also gives a remedy of not only avoiding them but also how to improve yourself to become a better advisor. I am so glad I read it, and I plan on reading it several times to make this stuff second nature. Thank you, Al for paving the way to become a great Financial Advisor.

Cheryl B., CFP

Al is such a wealth of information. Great place to start - understanding such a complex system. He shares his wisdom from years of personal experience. Love this book!

Terry M., CFP

Little mistakes in your Advisor business can cost you, clients! Great information regarding Medicare. Explains clearly what Part A and B covers plus much more. Do the little things correctly and retain and grow your client base!

Bill W., Investment Advisor

Whether you are new to the business or a seasoned professional... this book is a MUST-have! Thanks Al.

Sherry T., P&C Agent

You can be someone other than a financial advisor or investment representative to get value out of this book. Anyone working to preserve a client base will benefit from this book. It is written in short, relevant chapters. Many of the ideas are also expressed using stories as examples. Thanks for writing such a great book!

John W., Attorney

Al is a total pro at what he does; this book has helped me so much being young in the financial services world. So many valuable tips in this book!

Paula P., Investment Advisor

He does a great job of explaining the Medicare process and all of its choices clearly and concisely far better than any of the other books on the subject I've seen. Great advice from a proven professional and role model!

Rachel B., Insurance Agent

Outstanding book. Simple read with POWERFUL ideas. For those in financial services, buy this book in cases and give it to your team. Thank you Al ! Well Done :)

Harry S., CFP

Written so that you would understand no matter how many years you've been in the business—giving examples to visualize what he means in his explanations. This can add so much to your skills if you're newer (less than 10 yrs). The book is worth far more than the investment. So glad a friend recommended it.

Debra F., RIA

I highly recommend this book to anyone trying to understand and navigate the Medicare process. Easy to read and extremely helpful. I love how I can read and re-read this book in a single sitting and walk away with action points every time. Such tremendous value!!!

Mary P., CFP

This book came highly recommended by a good friend of mine. It is brilliant in its simplicity. Every financial professional, new and seasoned, will find powerful yet simple insights that, if implemented, will drastically increase their client satisfaction, continuing business, and great, new referrals. Even though I know a great deal about the Medicare process and have been participating for 3+ years, this book was excellent! By using the principles in this book, I will dramatically enhance my client relationships and increase my income in the years to come. I strongly encourage everyone in our agency to read this and implement the ideas ASAP!

Thomas H., CFA

I've read many books on Medicare, watched videos, talked with people, and was still confused, and then I bought this book. I went from clueless to confident in a short period. I can't recommend this enough. Advisors make mistakes that cost their clients thousands of dollars each year. If you don't know what you're doing, you can ruin your relationships in no time. Get the book!!

Roberta R., Financial Planner

Al's book is so well written that any advisor can benefit greatly from reading and studying this material. Even though I have done a lot of what Al says, I learned many things that I need to improve and implement ASAP. This book is required for all office staff and advisors who want to enhance their business significantly.

Alfred N., CFP

Coming from a career in financial services with a degree, I thought Medicare would be just another government run-around. How bad could it be? Well. It's the federal government at its best, second only to dealing with the IRS. This book is a road map through the government maze. Al has created a simple 10-chapter book you can read quickly and understand the process.

David Z., CPA

I bought this book a few months ago. I just ordered five more for my top producers. Al is a master at Medicare. I am grateful to have access to him and his experience. One of the best books I've ever read on how to educate your clients properly. I highly recommend this book to anyone serious about client retention and satisfaction.

Moishe V., General Agent

This is the best book I have ever read to help an advisor expand his knowledge about Medicare! Mr. Kushner's talent for putting a strategy together is easy to follow and an excellent read for new or older advisors. A definite "must read" for someone wanting to grow their business in today's environment. Thanks so much Al from a big fan!!

Dennis T., CFP

This book is FULL of helpful information for those getting ready to join Medicare. I was so confused before I read it, and now I understand how all the different plans work. So many choices out there, but this book will help you decide which way to go. I highlighted a lot of chapters for future reference, especially the ones explaining Part D drug coverage and possible penalties. Beneficial material! So glad I bought this book!

Denise Y., RIA

Table of Contents

INTRODUCTION

As a financial advisor, you play a crucial role in ensuring your clients have the resources they need to make informed decisions about their health and financial well-being. Medicare is a remarkably complex and ever-changing aspect of retirement planning, and it can be easy to fall into common mistakes that could have significant consequences for your clients.

That's why I wrote this book - 10 Medicare Mistakes Financial Advisors Make and How to Avoid Them. In it, I'll outline the top 10 mistakes financial advisors make when navigating Medicare and provide actionable steps for avoiding them. Whether you're a seasoned pro or just starting, this book will help you understand the Medicare system and avoid costly missteps that could impact your client's health and financial stability.

We know that Medicare can be overwhelming, with various coverage options, enrollment periods, and regulations to consider. That's why we've created this book - to help you simplify the process and ensure your clients have the coverage they need. From underestimating the complexity of Medicare to neglecting to consider Medicare Advantage plans, you'll learn about the pitfalls to avoid and gain a deeper understanding of the system.

My goal with this book is to provide you with the knowledge and resources you need to help your clients make informed decisions about Medicare. With real-world examples, expert insights, and practical tips, this book is your essential resource for ensuring your clients have the coverage they need. Don't let Medicare mistakes cost your clients their peace of mind.

This book's genesis is looking for ways to improve my skills and sharing what I have learned along the way. I compiled ten common mistakes and the simple, commonsense solutions to overcome them. Avoid common pitfalls and give your clients the security they deserve with 10 Medicare Mistakes Financial Advisors Make and How to Avoid Them.

One note about terminology: I use the title financial advisor throughout this book. I do it because it is the title generally used by clients, Finra, the sec, and the Department of Labor. As well as, of course, numerous other professional designations for those providing advisory services.

These include:

▶ Accountants

▶ Certified Public Accountants

▶ Chartered Financial Analyst

▶ Chartered Financial Consultant

▶ Certified Financial Planner

▶ Divorce Attorneys

▶ Elder Law Attorneys

▶ Estate Attorneys

▶ Financial Planner

▶ Investment Advisor Representative

▶ Investment Advisor

▶ Personal Financial Specialist

▶ Registered Rep

▶ Registered Investment Advisor

I am a licensed insurance broker. No matter your title or professional designation, I hope you understand better how to minimize mistakes and improve the overall client experience.

CHAPTER 1:

Underestimating The Complexity of Medicare

As a financial advisor, it's easy to think of Medicare as just another insurance program, but the reality is that it's much more complex than that. Unfortunately, many financial advisors make the mistake of underestimating the complexity of Medicare and giving their clients incomplete or incorrect advice. In this chapter, we'll explore why Medicare is so complex and discuss strategies for avoiding the common mistakes financial advisors make when dealing with it.

One of the biggest challenges of Medicare is that it has multiple parts, each of which covers different types of medical services. For example, part A covers inpatient hospital stays, skilled nursing facilities, and some home health care services. There's Part B, which covers doctor visits, medical equipment, and outpatient procedures. And there's Part D, which covers prescription drugs. Each Part of Medicare has its own set of rules, costs, and coverage limitations, making it difficult to understand what is and isn't covered by the program.

Another factor contributing to Medicare's complexity is its different enrollment periods and deadlines. For example, the initial enrollment period begins three months before your 65th birthday and lasts for seven months. There's also the annual open enrollment period, during which you can change your coverage. It's essential to understand when these enrollment periods occur and what you need to do during each one, or you may miss out on critical coverage options.

Finally, it's essential to understand that Medicare doesn't cover everything. There are still many out-of-pocket expenses that you'll need to pay for, even if you have Medicare. For example, you'll typically have to pay a deductible for each hospital stay and a coinsurance for each day you're in the hospital. You'll also have to pay a premium for Part B coverage and a monthly premium for Part D if you enroll in a standalone prescription drug plan. All these costs can add up, so it's essential to clearly understand what you'll be responsible for and what your Medicare coverage will pay for.

So, how can you avoid the common mistakes that financial advisors make when dealing with Medicare? One strategy is to stay up-to-date on the latest Medicare news and changes. This can be done by subscribing to newsletters, attending

Medicare seminars, and visiting the Medicare website. It would be best to educate yourself on the different parts of Medicare and the coverage options available so that you can help your clients make informed decisions about their coverage.

Finally, it's essential to communicate openly and honestly with your clients about their Medicare coverage and what they can expect to pay for out-of-pocket. Doing these things can help your clients make the most of their Medicare coverage and avoid the common mistakes that many financial advisors make.

CHAPTER 2:

Failing to Plan for Medicare Enrollment

As a financial advisor, one of the biggest mistakes you can make is failing to plan for your clients' Medicare enrollment. This is crucial as they transition from private insurance to a government-run program. Unfortunately, many financial advisors need to pay more attention to the importance of this transition and take the time to help their clients prepare for it. In this chapter, we'll explore why this is such a common mistake and provide some tips for avoiding it.

One of the reasons why failing to plan for Medicare enrollment is such a common mistake is that many financial advisors assume it's a straightforward process. After all, everyone is eligible for Medicare when they turn 65. While that may be true, there's much more to it than just turning 65 and enrolling in the program. For example, there are different enrollment periods and deadlines that you need to be aware of, and there are other coverage options available, each with its own set of rules and costs. Unfortunately, if you're still familiar with these things, you could give your clients incorrect or incomplete advice.

Another reason failing to plan for Medicare enrollment is a common mistake is that many financial advisors don't understand the impact that Medicare will have on their client's finances. Medicare is not a one-size-fits-all program, and the costs and coverage can vary greatly depending on the coverage options that your clients choose. For example, suppose your client enrolls in a Medicare Advantage plan instead of traditional Medicare. In that case, they may have lower out-of-pocket costs, but they'll also be limited in terms of the medical services they can receive. If you need help understanding these trade-offs and how they'll impact your client's finances, you could be doing them a disservice.

So, how can you avoid failing to plan for Medicare enrollment? The first step is to educate yourself on the different parts of Medicare and available coverage options. This will help you understand each option's costs and coverage limitations so that you can help your clients make informed decisions about their coverage. Next, it's essential to communicate with your clients about their Medicare enrollment so that you can help them understand the different options available to them and what they can expect to pay for out-of-pocket. Lastly, it would help if you worked with your clients to create a comprehensive plan for their Medicare enrollment, considering their current financial situation, health needs, and long-term goals.

Navigating Medicare and Health Savings Accounts (HSAs)

As a financial advisor, you play a crucial role in helping your clients understand how Medicare may impact different aspects of their financial lives. Unfortunately, one area that can often be confusing is the relationship between Medicare and Health Savings Accounts (HSAs). Here is where we'll explore the impact of Medicare on HSAs, and provide you with the information you need to help your clients make informed decisions about their HSA and Medicare coverage.

1. What is an HSA? A Health Savings Account (HSA) is a type of savings account that allows your clients to set aside pre-tax dollars to pay for eligible healthcare expenses. HSAs are often paired with high-deductible health plans (HDHPs) and are designed to help your clients save money on

healthcare costs while also helping them save on taxes.

2. When Can Your Clients Enroll in Medicare? Your clients can enroll in Medicare when they turn 65 or if they're under 65 and receiving Social Security Disability Insurance (SSDI) benefits. If your clients have an HSA and are nearing Medicare eligibility, it's essential to understand how Medicare will impact their HSA.

3. What Happens to Your Clients' HSA When They Enroll in Medicare? Once your clients enroll in Medicare, they can no longer contribute to their HSA. Additionally, they will no longer be able to use their HSA funds to pay for many of the expenses that Medicare covers. However, they may still be able to use their HSA funds to pay for certain healthcare

expenses that Medicare, such as deductibles, copayments, and coinsurance, do not cover.

4. Exploring Medicare Supplement and Medicare Advantage Options In some cases, your clients may choose to enroll in a Medicare Supplement (Medigap) plan or a Medicare Advantage plan. Both options may impact your clients' HSA in different ways, so it's essential to understand the implications of each choice.

For example, if your client enrolls in a Medicare Supplement plan, they may still be able to use their HSA funds to pay for certain out-of-pocket expenses. On the other hand, if your client enrolls in a Medicare Advantage plan, they may no longer be able to use their HSA funds to pay for many healthcare expenses, as these plans often have more comprehensive coverage.

1. The Importance of Communication and Planning, the relationship between Medicare and HSAs, can be complex. Still, with proper communication and planning, you can help your clients navigate this landscape and make informed decisions about their healthcare coverage. Encourage your clients to consider their HSA and Medicare coverage options well before their Medicare eligibility date and ensure they have all the information they need to make an informed decision.

By staying up-to-date on the latest Medicare and HSA regulations and providing your clients with clear and comprehensive information, you can help them make the best decisions for their healthcare coverage and financial well-being.

In conclusion, failing to plan for Medicare enrollment is a common mistake that financial advisors make, but it can easily be avoided. By educating yourself on the different parts of Medicare, communicating with your clients about their enrollment options, and creating a comprehensive plan for their enrollment, you can help your clients make the most of their Medicare coverage and avoid the common mistakes that many financial advisors make.

CHAPTER 3:

Ignoring the Different Parts of Medicare

A s a financial advisor, one of the biggest mistakes you can make when it comes to Medicare is ignoring the different parts of the program. Medicare is a complex system comprising several factors, each with its rules, coverage, and costs. If you don't understand the different parts of Medicare, you could give your clients incorrect or incomplete advice. In this chapter, we'll explore the other parts of Medicare and why it's so important for financial advisors to understand them.

The first Part of Medicare is Part A, which provides hospital insurance. This Part of Medicare covers hospital stays, nursing, and hospice care. Part A is generally free for most people, but there are certain circumstances where a person may have to pay a premium for Part A coverage. Therefore, financial advisors need to understand Part A because it affects how much their clients will pay out-of-pocket for hospital care.

The second Part of Medicare is Part B, which provides medical insurance. Part B covers doctor visits, diagnostic tests, and medical equipment. Part B is not free, and a monthly premium must be paid for this coverage. Additionally, a deductible must be met before Part B coverage kicks in. Financial advisors need to understand Part B because it affects how much their clients will pay for medical services and how much they will be responsible for out-of-pocket.

The third Part of Medicare is Part C, also known as Medicare Advantage. Private insurance companies offer Medicare Advantage plans and provide an alternative to traditional Medicare. These plans typically offer a more comprehensive coverage package than traditional Medicare, but they can also be more expensive. As a result, financial advisors need to understand Medicare Advantage plans because they can be a good option for clients who want more comprehensive coverage but may not want to pay the higher costs associated with traditional Medicare.

The fourth Part of Medicare is Part D, which provides prescription drug coverage. Part D is not automatically included with Medicare coverage and must be purchased separately. Part D plans can vary significantly in terms of the drugs they cover and the costs they charge, so financial advisors need to understand Part D to help their clients choose the best plan for their needs.

In conclusion, ignoring the different parts of Medicare is a common mistake that financial advisors make, but it can be easily avoided. By understanding the other parts of Medicare, including Part A, Part B, Part C, and Part D, you can help your clients make informed decisions about their Medicare coverage and avoid the common mistakes many financial advisors make.

Whether you're helping a client choose between traditional Medicare and Medicare Advantage or helping them select a Part D plan, it's essential to understand the different parts of Medicare so you can provide your clients with the best possible advice.

CHAPTER 4:

Not Exploring All Medicare Coverage Options

As a financial advisor, one of your primary responsibilities is to help your clients make informed decisions about their Medicare coverage. This means exploring all available Medicare coverage options and helping your clients choose the option that is right for them. Unfortunately, many financial advisors make the mistake of not exploring all of the Medicare coverage options, leading to their clients missing out on coverage that could benefit them. In this chapter, we'll explore why it's so important for financial advisors to investigate all Medicare coverage options and what options are available.

One of the biggest reasons why financial advisors need to explore all Medicare coverage options is that Medicare coverage is not a one-size-fits-all proposition. Financial advisors need to understand that what works for one client may not. By exploring all of the available Medicare coverage options, you can help your clients find the coverage that is right for them and ensure that they are not missing out on coverage that could benefit them.

So what options are available when it comes to Medicare coverage? The first option is traditional Medicare, comprised of Part A and Part B. This option is a fee-for-service option that allows clients to see any doctor or hospital that accepts Medicare. While this option provides a lot of flexibility, it can also be more expensive than other options, as clients are responsible for paying a portion of the costs associated with their medical care.

Another option is Medicare Advantage, also known as Part C. Medicare Advantage plans are offered by private insurance companies and provide an alternative to traditional Medicare. These plans typically offer a more comprehensive coverage package than traditional Medicare, but they can also be more expensive. Therefore, financial advisors need to understand Medicare Advantage plans because they can be a good option for clients who want more comprehensive coverage but may not want to pay the higher costs associated with traditional Medicare.

In addition to traditional Medicare and Medicare Advantage, there are also Medicare Supplement plans. These plans are designed to fill in the gaps left by traditional Medicare, and they can help clients pay for things like deductibles, copays, and coinsurance. Private insurance companies offer

Medicare Supplement plans. They can be a good option for clients who want more comprehensive coverage but do not want to enroll in a Medicare Advantage plan.

Finally, there is Medicare Part D, which provides prescription drug coverage. Part D is not automatically included with Medicare coverage, and it must be purchased separately. Part D plans can vary significantly in terms of the drugs they cover and the costs they charge, so financial advisors need to understand Part D to help their clients choose the best plan for their needs.

In conclusion, not exploring all Medicare coverage options is a common mistake that financial advisors make, but it can be easily avoided. By analyzing all of the available Medicare coverage options, including traditional Medicare, Medicare Advantage, Medicare Supplement plans, and Medicare Part D, you can help your clients find the coverage that is right for them and ensure that they are not missing out on range that could be beneficial to them.

So whether you're helping a client choose between traditional Medicare and Medicare Advantage or helping them select a Part D plan, it's essential to explore all of the Medicare coverage options so you can provide your clients with the best possible advice.

CHAPTER 5:

Misunderstanding Medicare Supplement Plans

As a financial advisor, it's essential to understand the various options available for Medicare coverage, including Medicare Supplement plans. Unfortunately, many financial advisors need to understand these plans, which can lead to their clients missing out on valuable coverage. In this chapter, we'll explore the key features of Medicare Supplement plans and why they are essential for financial advisors to understand.

First, it's essential to understand what a Medicare Supplement plan is. Also known as Medigap, Medicare Supplement plans are designed to fill in the gaps left by traditional Medicare. These plans help pay for deductibles, copays, and coinsurance, which helps reduce out-of-pocket costs for clients. Private insurance companies offer Medicare Supplement plans, which are available to individuals enrolled in traditional Medicare.

One of the biggest misunderstandings about Medicare Supplement plans is that they are all the same. This is not true. Ten different Medicare Supplement plans are available, each with its coverage options. Some programs may cover deductibles, while others may not. Some may cover copays, while others may not. It's vital for financial advisors to understand the different Medicare Supplement plans and what they cover so they can help their clients choose the program that is right for them.

Another misunderstanding about Medicare Supplement plans is that they are too expensive. While it's true that Medicare Supplement plans can be more costly than traditional Medicare, they can also provide more comprehensive coverage. Therefore, financial advisors need to understand the costs associated with Medicare Supplement plans to help their clients decide whether this type of coverage is right for them.

It's also essential for financial advisors to understand that Medicare Supplement plans are not automatically included with Medicare coverage. Instead, clients must enroll in a Medicare Supplement plan separately and be enrolled in traditional Medicare to be eligible for this type of coverage. Financial advisors must understand this to help their clients enroll in the right coverage at the right time.

Finally, financial advisors must understand that Medicare Supplement plans have open enrollment periods. Clients can enroll in a Medicare Supplement plan during these periods without answering medical questions. This is an essential feature of Medicare Supplement plans because it allows clients to register even with pre-existing medical conditions. Financial advisors must understand this to help their clients enroll in the right program at the right time, even if they have pre-existing medical conditions.

In conclusion, misunderstanding Medicare Supplement plans is a common mistake that financial advisors make, but it can be easily avoided. By understanding the key features of Medicare Supplement plans, including what they cover, their costs, how they are enrolled, and the open enrollment periods, financial advisors can help their clients make informed decisions about their Medicare coverage.

Whether you're helping a client choose between traditional Medicare and a Medicare Supplement plan or helping them understand their coverage options, it's essential to have a good understanding of Medicare Supplement plans so you can provide your clients with the best possible advice.

CHAPTER 6:

Underestimating the Cost of Medicare

As a financial advisor, it's essential to understand the costs associated with Medicare coverage, as these costs can significantly impact your clients' retirement plans. Unfortunately, many financial advisors make the mistake of underestimating the cost of Medicare, which can lead to their clients facing unexpected expenses in retirement. In this chapter, we'll explore the critical costs associated with Medicare and why financial advisors need to understand these costs.

First, it's essential to understand that Medicare has two primary costs: premiums and out-of-pocket costs. Premiums are the monthly fees that your clients pay to enroll in Medicare coverage. Out-of-pocket costs are the costs that your clients pay when they receive medical services, such as deductibles, copays, and coinsurance. These costs can add up quickly, and financial advisors must understand the total cost of Medicare coverage to help their clients plan accordingly.

One of the biggest mistakes financial advisors make is underestimating the cost of premiums. Premiums can be expensive, especially for clients who are enrolled in Medicare Advantage plans. Therefore, financial advisors need to understand the cost of tips to help their clients budget accordingly and make informed decisions about their Medicare coverage.

Another cost that is often underestimated is the cost of out-of-pocket expenses. While traditional Medicare does provide coverage for a wide range of medical services, it does not cover everything. Clients may be responsible for paying deductibles, copays, and coinsurance, which can add up quickly. Financial advisors need to understand these costs to help their clients budget for them and make informed decisions about their Medicare coverage.

It's also essential for financial advisors to understand the cost of prescription drugs. Prescription drugs can be expensive, and many Medicare clients will need to enroll in a separate drug plan to receive coverage for these costs. Therefore, financial advisors need to understand the cost of prescription drugs to help their clients budget for this expense and make informed decisions about their Medicare coverage.

As a financial advisor, knowing about all the different options available to your clients regarding Medicare coverage is essential. Unfortunately, one area that is often overlooked is the Medicare Savings Program. Below we'll explore the different types of Medicare Savings Programs and what they offer.

1. Qualified Medicare Beneficiary (QMB) Program: The Qualified Medicare Beneficiary (QMB) Program is designed to help low-income Medicare beneficiaries pay for their Medicare Part A and Part B premiums and their deductibles, coinsurance, and copayments. To be eligible for this program, beneficiaries must have an income that is less than or equal to the federal poverty level.

2. Specified Low-Income Medicare Beneficiary (SLMB) Program: The Specified Low-Income Medicare Beneficiary (SLMB) Program is similar to the QMB Program in that it helps low-income Medicare beneficiaries pay for their Medicare Part B

premiums. However, unlike the QMB Program, the SLMB Program does not cover deductibles, coinsurance, and copayments. To be eligible for this program, beneficiaries must have an income that is less than or equal to the federal poverty level but above the QMB Program's income limit.

3. Qualifying Individual (QI) Program: The Qualifying Individual (QI) Program is designed to help Medicare beneficiaries pay for their Medicare Part B premiums. To be eligible for this program, beneficiaries must have an income that is less than or equal to the federal poverty level and must also be enrolled in Medicare Part B. The federal government funds this program, and the amount of assistance that beneficiaries receive can vary yearly based on funding availability.

4. Qualified Disabled and Working Individuals (QDWI) Program: The Qualified Disabled and Working Individuals (QDWI) Program is designed to help individuals who are disabled and working to pay for their Medicare Part A premiums. To be eligible for this program, beneficiaries must have a disability, be working, and be enrolled in Medicare Part A. The federal government funds this program, and the amount of assistance that beneficiaries receive can vary yearly based on funding availability.

It's important to note that eligibility for these programs can vary depending on the state in which you reside. Additionally, the rules and regulations surrounding these programs can change yearly, so it's crucial to stay up-to-date on the latest information.

The Medicare Savings Program can be a valuable resource for low-income Medicare beneficiaries struggling to pay for their Medicare coverage. By understanding the different types of Medicare Savings Programs and what they offer, financial advisors can help their clients explore all the options available regarding Medicare coverage.

Whether your clients are struggling to pay for their Medicare Part A and Part B premiums or need assistance paying for their deductibles, coinsurance, and copayments, the Medicare Savings Programs can provide valuable support and help ensure that they have access to the coverage they need.

Exploring Assistance Programs for Medicare Costs

As a financial advisor, it's essential to be knowledgeable about all the different options available to your clients when it comes to paying for their Medicare costs. Below we'll explore four assistance programs that could help your clients pay their Medicare costs and provide the coverage they need.

1. Medicaid is a joint federal and state program that provides health coverage to low-income individuals and families. In some states, Medicaid can help cover the cost of Medicare premiums, deductibles, coinsurance, and copayments. In addition, Medicaid can also provide additional benefits that Medicare, such as long-term care services, does not cover. To be eligible for Medicaid, beneficiaries must have an income less than or equal to the federal poverty level.

2. Extra Help: The Extra Help program, also known as the Low-Income Subsidy (LIS), is designed to help Medicare beneficiaries pay for their prescription drug costs. To be eligible for this program, beneficiaries must have an income that is less than or equal to the federal poverty level and must also have limited resources. The Extra Help program can assist beneficiaries with paying for their prescription drug

premiums, deductibles, coinsurance, and copayments.

3. Medicare Savings Programs are designed to help low-income Medicare beneficiaries pay for their Medicare Part A and Part B premiums and their deductibles, coinsurance, and copayments. There are four types of Medicare Savings Programs, each with its eligibility requirements.

4. Veterans Benefits: For veterans and their dependents, the Department of Veterans Affairs (VA) offers a variety of healthcare benefits that can help cover the cost of Medicare. These benefits include comprehensive health care coverage, prescription drug coverage, and assistance paying for Medicare premiums and other expenses. To be eligible for these benefits veterans must meet

specific eligibility requirements, such as having served on active duty and enrolled in Medicare.

It's important to note that eligibility for these programs can vary depending on the state in which you reside. Additionally, the rules and regulations surrounding these programs can change yearly, so staying up-to-date on the latest information is essential.

These assistance programs can provide valuable support for Medicare beneficiaries who are struggling to pay for their Medicare costs. By understanding the different options available, financial advisors can help their clients explore all available options and ensure they have access to the coverage they need. Whether your clients need help paying for their Medicare premiums, deductibles, coinsurance, or copayments, these assistance programs can provide the support they need and help ensure they have access to the health care coverage they need.

Finally, financial advisors need to understand the cost of long-term care. Long-term care can be expensive, and Medicare does not cover all of these costs. Clients may need to enroll in a separate long-term care insurance policy to receive coverage for these costs. Financial advisors need to understand the cost of long-term care to help their clients budget for this expense and make informed decisions about their Medicare coverage.

In conclusion, underestimating the cost of Medicare is a common mistake that financial advisors make, but it can be easily avoided. By understanding the essential costs associated with Medicare, including premiums, out-of-pocket expenses, prescription drugs, and long-term care, financial advisors can help their clients plan for these costs and make informed decisions about their Medicare coverage.

Whether you're helping a client budget for Medicare costs or helping them choose between different coverage options, it's essential to understand the costs associated with Medicare so

you can provide your clients with the best possible advice.

CHAPTER 7:

Neglecting to Consider Medicare Advantage Plans

As a financial advisor, knowing about all the options available to your clients regarding Medicare coverage is essential. Unfortunately, many financial advisors make the mistake of neglecting to consider Medicare Advantage plans, which can be a missed opportunity for their clients. This chapter will explore what Medicare Advantage plans are and why they should be considered for your clients.

Medicare Advantage plans, also known as Medicare Part C, are private health insurance plans that Medicare approves. They provide a comprehensive range of medical benefits, including hospital stays, doctor visits, and prescription drug coverage. Medicare Advantage plans are an alternative to traditional Medicare and are designed to provide clients with a more comprehensive and convenient healthcare experience.

One of the reasons that financial advisors may neglect to consider Medicare Advantage plans is that they don't understand how these plans work. Many financial advisors are familiar with traditional Medicare, but they may not understand the differences between traditional Medicare and Medicare Advantage plans. Financial advisors must understand these differences to make informed recommendations to their clients.

Another reason that financial advisors may neglect to consider Medicare Advantage plans is that they believe they are more expensive than traditional Medicare. While this can be true in some cases, it's essential to understand that Medicare Advantage plans often include benefits that conventional Medicare, such as dental and vision coverage, do not cover. In many cases, these extra benefits can offset the higher costs of the Medicare Advantage plan.

Financial advisors may also neglect to consider Medicare Advantage plans because they believe they have more restrictions on the choice of healthcare providers. While this can be true in some cases, it's essential to understand that many Medicare Advantage plans have a network of providers, just like traditional Medicare. In many cases, these networks are just as significant as those offered by traditional Medicare, and clients can choose from a wide range of healthcare providers.

Financial advisors may neglect to consider Medicare Advantage plans because they believe they are more complicated than traditional Medicare. While this can be true in some cases, it's essential to understand that Medicare Advantage plans are designed to be user-friendly. In addition, many of these plans offer tools and resources to help clients navigate the program and make informed decisions about their healthcare.

As a financial advisor, you must help your clients understand the options available to them regarding Medicare coverage. One way to evaluate other possibilities is through Medicare's 5-Star Rating System. This system rates Medicare Advantage plans and prescription drug plans on a scale of one to five stars, with five stars being the highest rating. This chapter will explore the Medicare 5-Star Rating System and what it means for your clients.

The Medicare 5-Star Rating System is designed to help consumers evaluate and compare different Medicare Advantage and prescription drug plans. The system considers several factors, including the quality of care that the program provides, the cost of the project, and customer satisfaction. The ratings are updated annually, so it's essential to check the latest ratings before making a coverage decision.

One of the benefits of the Medicare 5-Star Rating System is that it provides a quick and easy way for consumers to compare different options. By comparing the ratings of other plans, consumers can get a sense of the quality of care each program provides and the plan's cost. This information can be beneficial for consumers who are new to Medicare or who are looking to make a change to their current coverage.

Another benefit of the Medicare 5-Star Rating System is that it can help consumers make informed decisions about their coverage. By understanding the quality of care a plan provides, consumers can make decisions about their coverage that align with their health needs and goals. Additionally, consumers can make decisions within their budget by understanding the plan's cost.

However, it's essential to understand that the Medicare 5-Star Rating System is just one tool for evaluating different Medicare coverage options. While the ratings can provide a helpful starting point, it's essential to dig deeper and assess the specifics of each plan before making a coverage decision. For example, you may find that a program with a lower rating provides better coverage for a specific health condition or that a plan with a higher rating is not the best option for a client's budget.

It's also important to remember that the Medicare 5-Star Rating System is updated annually, so it's essential to check the latest ratings before making a coverage decision. This is particularly important for clients already enrolled in a Medicare Advantage or prescription drug plan, as the ratings can change yearly.

The Medicare 5-Star Rating System is valuable for evaluating different Medicare coverage options. Clients can make informed decisions about their Medicare coverage by understanding the quality of care that a plan provides and the project's cost. As a financial advisor, it's vital to help your clients understand the Medicare 5-Star Rating System and how it can be used to evaluate different coverage options. Whether your clients are new to Medicare or looking to change their current coverage, the Medicare 5-Star Rating System can be a valuable tool for helping them make informed decisions about their Medicare coverage.

In conclusion, neglecting to consider Medicare Advantage plans is a common mistake that financial advisors make, but it can be easily avoided. By understanding the benefits of these plans, including comprehensive benefits, extra benefits, and user-friendly design, financial advisors can help their clients make informed decisions about their Medicare coverage.

Whether you're helping a client choose between different coverage options or helping them understand the benefits of a Medicare Advantage plan, it's essential to have a good understanding of these plans to provide your clients with the best possible advice.

CHAPTER 8:

Overlooking the Importance of Prescription Drug Coverage

As a financial advisor, you must understand the importance of prescription drug coverage for your clients. But unfortunately, many financial advisors need to pay more attention to the extent of this coverage, which can lead to unexpected costs and financial burdens for their clients. In this chapter, we'll explore the importance of prescription drug coverage and why it's a critical component of any Medicare coverage plan.

Prescription drug coverage is essential to healthcare, as many rely on prescription medications to manage their health conditions. Unfortunately, prescription drugs can be costly for some clients, and they can quickly become unaffordable without proper coverage. This is particularly true for those living on a fixed income or with limited financial resources.

One of the reasons that financial advisors may overlook the importance of prescription drug coverage is that they believe that their clients don't need this coverage. While this may be true for some clients, it's essential to understand that the need for prescription drugs can change over time. For example, a client who is healthy today may develop a health condition in the future that requires the use of prescription drugs. However, with proper coverage, this client may be able to handle unexpected and unaffordable costs.

Another reason that financial advisors may overlook the importance of prescription drug coverage because they believe that traditional Medicare covers these drugs. While conventional Medicare does provide some coverage for prescription drugs, it's essential to understand that this coverage is limited and may not be enough to meet a client's needs. In many cases, clients may need to purchase a separate prescription drug plan to ensure adequate coverage.

Prescription discount cards are one of the most straightforward ways for your clients to save money on their prescription drug costs. These cards are available from various sources and offer discounts of up to 50% or more on prescription drugs. Many Medicare Advantage and Medicare Supplement plans include a prescription drug plan, but prescription discount cards can be a lifesaver for those that don't.

Pharmaceutical assistance programs are another excellent way for your clients to save on prescription drug costs. These programs are designed to provide financial assistance to eligible individuals who need help paying for their prescription drugs. Various programs are available, including those sponsored by pharmaceutical companies, state governments, and non-profit organizations. To find out if your client is eligible for any of these programs, you can refer them to their local Area Agency on Aging or the Medicare website.

Another way your clients can save money on their Medicare costs is to be mindful of their out-of-pocket expenses. For example, they can save money by using generic drugs instead of brand-name drugs, shopping around for the best prices on medical equipment and supplies, and choosing providers who accept Medicare assignments.

Your clients can also save money on their Medicare costs by taking Advantage of various programs and services designed to help lower their prices. For example, they can enroll in the Medicare Savings Program, which provides financial assistance to eligible Medicare beneficiaries. They can also enroll in the Extra Help program, which assists with prescription drug costs for those with limited income and resources.

Your clients need to understand the different options available regarding prescription drug coverage. For example, they can enroll in a standalone prescription drug plan or choose a Medicare Advantage plan that includes prescription drug coverage. They should also be aware of the coverage gaps that can occur with prescription drug coverage and plan accordingly.

Finally, it's essential to encourage your clients to take an active role in their healthcare. This means asking questions, researching, and making informed decisions about their treatment options. For example, they can explore alternative treatments that may be less expensive than traditional medical treatments or choose to participate in clinical trials for new therapies.

There are many ways for your clients to save money on their Medicare costs. As a financial advisor, you play a critical role in helping them understand their options and make informed decisions about their healthcare. By staying informed about the latest money-saving Medicare tips, you can help your clients get the most out of their Medicare coverage while keeping their costs as low as possible.

In addition, by understanding prescription discount cards, pharmaceutical assistance programs, and other money-saving tips, you can help your clients make the most of their Medicare coverage and enjoy the peace of mind that comes with knowing they have access to the healthcare they need.

Overlooking the importance of prescription drug coverage is a common mistake that financial advisors make, but it can be easily avoided. By understanding the importance of prescription drug coverage, including the potential for unexpected costs, limited coverage under traditional Medicare, and the need for separate coverage plans, financial advisors can help their clients make informed decisions about their Medicare coverage.

Whether you're helping a client choose between different coverage options or helping them understand the benefits of a prescription drug plan, it's essential to have a good understanding of this coverage to provide your clients with the best possible advice.

CHAPTER 9:

Failing to Communicate with Clients about Medicare

As a financial advisor, it's essential to communicate effectively with your clients about their Medicare coverage. Unfortunately, many financial advisors fail to communicate effectively with their clients about Medicare, which can lead to confusion, misunderstandings, and suboptimal coverage decisions. In this chapter, we'll explore the importance of effective communication about Medicare and the consequences of failing to communicate effectively with your clients.

Effective communication is critical when it comes to Medicare coverage because Medicare is a complex and often confusing system. There are many parts to Medicare, and clients may not understand the options available to them. By failing to communicate effectively with your clients about Medicare, you risk missing the opportunity to help them make informed decisions about their coverage.

One of the reasons that financial advisors fail to communicate effectively with their clients about Medicare is because they believe their clients are not interested in this topic. While this may be true for some clients, it's essential to understand that many clients are concerned about their Medicare coverage and want to understand the options available. By assuming your clients are not interested in this topic, you risk missing the opportunity to help them make informed decisions about their coverage.

Another reason financial advisors fail to communicate effectively with their clients about Medicare is because they don't understand the system's complexity. Medicare is a complex system, and it can be challenging to understand the different parts and options available. By not understanding the system's complexity, financial advisors may struggle to communicate effectively with their clients about their Medicare coverage.

Financial advisors may also fail to communicate effectively with their clients about Medicare because they believe their clients have already made up their minds about their coverage. While this may be true for some clients, it's essential to understand that many are still exploring their options and may be open to different coverage options. By assuming that your clients have already made up their minds, you risk missing the opportunity to help them make informed decisions about their coverage.

Navigating Medicare When Your Client Moves

Moving can be a significant change, and it's essential to understand how it can affect your client's Medicare coverage. Below we'll explore what happens to Medicare when your client moves and what steps they need to take to ensure their coverage remains intact.

1. Moving Within the Same State If your client is moving within the same state, their Medicare coverage should not be affected. They can continue to see the same doctors and use the same hospitals they did before they moved. They'll also continue to receive the same benefits from their Medicare Part A and Part B coverage. However, if your client is enrolled in a Medicare Advantage Plan or a Medicare Supplement Plan, they may need to find a new plan in their new area that covers the healthcare providers and hospitals they need.

2. Moving to a New State If your client is moving to a new state, they will need to take a few extra steps to ensure that their Medicare coverage remains intact. First, they'll need to notify Medicare of their change of address so that their records can be updated. They'll also need to determine if their current Medicare Advantage Plan or Medicare Supplement Plan is available in their new state. If it's not, they'll need to find a new plan that covers the health care providers and hospitals they need. In some cases, your client may also be eligible to enroll in a different Medicare Savings Program if they have a low income and are struggling to pay their Medicare costs.

3. Traveling Outside the U.S. If your client is traveling outside the U.S., their Medicare coverage will not follow them. Medicare does not cover health care services received outside the U.S. unless it's an emergency. Your client may need supplemental

insurance to cover any health care costs they may incur while traveling abroad.

It's important to note that if your client is enrolled in a Medicare Advantage Plan or a Medicare Supplement Plan, they may have additional coverage options available to them when they travel outside the U.S. You can help your client explore these options and determine the best course of action to ensure they have the coverage they need while they are abroad.

Moving can significantly impact your client's Medicare coverage. Whether they are moving within the same state, to a new state, or traveling outside the U.S., it's vital to help them understand the steps they need to take to ensure their coverage remains intact. By doing so, you can help them avoid any interruptions in their healthcare coverage and provide the support they need to stay healthy and comfortable.

Financial advisors may fail to communicate effectively with their clients about Medicare because they are uncomfortable with it. For some financial advisors, Medicare may not be their area of expertise, and they may be uncomfortable discussing this topic with their clients. By being uncomfortable with the subject, financial advisors may avoid discussing Medicare with their clients, which can lead to misunderstandings and suboptimal coverage decisions.

Helping Your Clients Get a Medicare Authorized Representative

As a financial advisor, it's essential to help your clients navigate the complexities of the Medicare system, including getting a Medicare Authorized Representative (MAR). A MAR is a Medicare recipient and has designated an individual to represent them in dealing with Medicare-related matters, such as enrolling in a Medicare plan or handling appeals for denied claims.

Having a MAR can be especially helpful for clients struggling to understand the Medicare system, dealing with a severe medical condition, or simply wanting an extra hand to handle their Medicare-related needs. Here's how you can help your clients get a MAR:

1. Explain the importance of a MAR: Explain to your client what a MAR is and why having one can be helpful. Discuss the benefits, such as having someone who can help them enroll in a Medicare plan, handle appeals, and communicate with Medicare on their behalf.

2. Help find a MAR: There are several ways to find a MAR. You can start by searching the Medicare website or contacting Medicare directly. Another option is to work with a local elder law attorney who can recommend a MAR in your area.

3. Understand the responsibilities of a MAR: Before your client designates a MAR, they must understand the role's responsibilities. A MAR must act by your client's wishes, keep their information confidential, and be able to handle Medicare-related matters on their behalf.

4. Complete the necessary forms: To designate a MAR, your client must complete the appropriate arrangements. You can help your client fill out the forms, ensure all the required information is included, and submit the documents to Medicare for processing.

5. Follow up: After your client has designated a MAR, it's essential to follow up and make sure that the MAR can handle the tasks that your client needs them to do. This may include enrolling in a Medicare

plan, handling appeals, or communicating with Medicare on their behalf.

By helping your clients get a MAR, you can give them peace of mind and help ease the stress of navigating the Medicare system. As a trusted financial advisor, you play an essential role in helping your clients navigate the complexities of Medicare, and getting a MAR is one way to do just that.

In conclusion, failing to communicate effectively with your clients about Medicare is a common mistake that financial advisors make, but it can be easily avoided. By understanding the importance of effective communication about Medicare, including the complexity of the system, the importance of client engagement, and the potential for misunderstandings, financial advisors can help their clients make informed decisions about their Medicare coverage.

Whether you're helping a client understand the different parts of Medicare or helping them choose between other coverage options, it's essential to communicate effectively to

provide your clients with the best possible advice.

CHAPTER 10:

Not Staying Up-to-Date on Medicare Changes and Updates

As a financial advisor, staying up-to-date on the latest Medicare changes and updates is essential. Unfortunately, many financial advisors must keep up-to-date on these changes, which can lead to misunderstandings and suboptimal coverage decisions for their clients. This chapter will explore the importance of staying up-to-date on Medicare changes and updates and the consequences of not doing so.

Medicare is a constantly evolving system, with changes and updates happening regularly. These changes can significantly impact your clients' coverage and their decisions about their Medicare coverage. For example, changes to the cost of premiums, deductibles, and copays can affect your clients' monthly expenses. In addition, changes to the types of services covered by Medicare can impact your clients' care.

Not staying up-to-date on the latest Medicare changes and updates makes financial advisors risk missing crucial information that could impact their clients' coverage decisions. This can lead to misunderstandings and suboptimal coverage decisions, which can be costly for your clients in the long run.

One of the reasons that financial advisors don't stay up-to-date on Medicare changes and updates is that they believe these changes won't impact their clients. While this may be true for some clients, it's essential to understand that these changes will affect many clients, and they want to know how they will impact their coverage. Therefore, you need to stay up-to-date on these changes to ensure you can help your clients make informed decisions about their coverage.

Another reason that financial advisors don't stay up-to-date on Medicare changes and updates because they don't have the time to do so. Between meeting with clients, managing portfolios, and staying up-to-date on other financial topics, it can be challenging to find the time to keep up-to-date on Medicare changes and updates. However, it's essential to stay up-to-date on these changes, as they can significantly impact your clients' coverage and their decisions about their Medicare coverage.

Finally, financial advisors may not stay up-to-date on Medicare changes and updates because they believe they already know all vital information. While having a solid understanding of Medicare is essential, it's also important to stay up-to-date on the latest changes and updates. Assuming you already know all the vital information, you risk missing important updates that could impact your clients' coverage decisions.

Does Medicare Coverage Change if Your Clients Return to Work?

As a financial advisor, it's essential to keep your clients informed about the impact of their decisions on their Medicare coverage. For example, one common question is whether Medicare coverage changes if a client returns to work. The answer is yes, it can, but the specifics depend on several factors.

First, it's essential to understand that Medicare is a federal health insurance program for people 65 or older, people with specific disabilities, and people with End-Stage Renal

Disease (ESRD). Medicare is designed to help pay for health care costs, but it does not cover all costs.

If a client is working and receiving a salary, they may be able to delay enrolling in Medicare. As a result, they can continue receiving health insurance through their employer, and they won't have to pay a late enrollment penalty when they enroll in Medicare later.

However, clients who have already enrolled in Medicare should be aware that their Medicare coverage could change if they return to work. If they have Medicare Part A (hospital insurance) and Medicare Part B (medical insurance), they may be able to keep their coverage. However, if they have a Medicare Advantage Plan, they will need to check with their plan to see if they can keep it while working.

If a client returns to work and is offered employer-sponsored health insurance, they may have to choose between their employer's insurance and their Medicare coverage. If their employer's insurance is a group health plan and has 20 or more employees, the employer's insurance is considered "creditable coverage." This means that it's as good as or better than Medicare coverage, and a client can use it instead of Medicare.

Suppose a client decides to use their employer's insurance. In that case, they should enroll in Medicare as soon as their employment ends or their employer's insurance is no longer considered "creditable." If they don't enroll in Medicare within eight months after their work ends, they may have to pay a late enrollment penalty when registering.

It's important to remember that even if a client is using their employer's insurance, they should still keep their Medicare card with them. This is because they may need it if they have to go to a hospital or doctor who doesn't take their employer's insurance.

Whether Medicare coverage changes if a client returns to work depends on several factors, including the type of Medicare coverage and the type of health insurance offered by their employer. As a financial advisor, you must educate your clients on these factors and help them make informed decisions about their health insurance coverage.

In conclusion, not staying up-to-date on Medicare changes and updates is a common mistake that financial advisors make, but it can be easily avoided. By understanding the importance of staying up-to-date on these changes and making the time to do so, financial advisors can help their clients make informed decisions about their Medicare coverage.

Whether you're helping a client understand the latest changes to their coverage options or helping them navigate the latest updates to the Medicare system, it's essential to stay up-to-date on these changes to provide your clients with

the best possible advice.

CONCLUSION

As a financial advisor, it's essential to have a thorough understanding of Medicare and how it impacts your clients. The decisions made around Medicare enrollment and coverage can have a significant impact on a client's financial future. In this book, we explored 10 common mistakes that financial advisors make when it comes to Medicare, and how to avoid them.

From underestimating the complexity of Medicare and failing to plan for enrollment, to ignoring the different parts of Medicare and not exploring all coverage options, we've covered some of the most significant areas where advisors can go wrong. We also looked at how important it is to stay up-to-date on changes and updates to Medicare, and the impact that enrolling in Medicare can have on a client's Health Savings Account (HSA).

The ultimate goal of this book is to equip financial advisors with the knowledge and understanding they need to make informed decisions for their clients. By avoiding these 10 common mistakes, you can help your clients navigate the Medicare landscape with confidence and ensure that their future is secure.

In conclusion, it's essential to remember that Medicare is a complex system, and it's crucial to approach it with caution. By taking the time to understand the different parts of Medicare, explore all coverage options, and stay up-to-date on changes, you can help your clients make informed decisions and avoid the costly mistakes that can impact their financial future.

I hope that you have found the ideas presented thought-provoking and will incorporate the appropriate simple ideas and best-practice actions into your business. Finally, I'll leave you with what has become my mantra for creating happy, loyal clients: Take care of your clients, or your competitors will.

RESOURCES

Centers for Medicare & Medicaid Services www.cms.gov

Medicare www.medicare.gov

Teladoc www.teladochealth.com

MDLive www.mdlnext.mdlive.com

Doctor on Demand www.doctorondemand.com

LiveHealth www.Livehealthonline.com

PlushCare www.PlushCare.com

Webex www.Webex.com

Apply for Medicare www.SSA.gov

Online Pharmacy www.Costplusdrugs.com

Discount Pharmacy www.EaglePharmacy.com

Patient Drug Assistance www.Abbvie.com

Patient Drug Assistance www.AZandMe.com

Patient Drug Assistance www.Gene.com

Patient Drug Assistance www.GSKforyou.com

Patient Drug Assistance www.RxPathways.com

Patient Drug Assistance www.Amgenassist360.com

Patient Drug Assistance www.Needymeds.org

Patient Drug Assistance www.Matorg.com

Patient Drug Assistance www.MyGooddays.org

Patient Drug Assistance www.TAFCares.org

Patient Drug Assistance www.Advocatemymeds.com

Independent Medicare Broker Al Kushner 888-810-9725

www.RealEasyMedicare.com

Essential Forms for Medicare & Social Security

www. MedicareForms.help

File A Medicare Claim

Application For Enrollment in Medicare Part B

Application For Termination of Medicare Part A and/or Part B

Enroll in Medicare Easy Pay - Automatic Premium Withdrawal

File A Complaint About The Quality of Healthcare You Received

Income Related Monthly Adjustment (IRMAA) Appeal

Proof of Creditable Coverage When Applying for Medicar

QUESTIONS FOR THE AUTHOR

What services do you offer for financial planners?

Our firm offers a comprehensive range of services, particularly on Medicare. We understand that navigating the complexities of Medicare can be challenging, and our goal is to simplify this process for our clients.

Our primary service involves providing personalized Medicare guidance. We assist individuals new to Medicare to understand its various parts - Part A, B, C, and D - and help them determine the most suitable plan according to their health needs and financial situation. We also provide ongoing support to ensure our clients get the most out of their Medicare benefits.

In addition, we guide clients through the annual enrollment or any necessary changes in their Medicare plan due to alterations in their health status or the availability of new plans. We aim to ensure our clients have the best possible healthcare coverage as they age.

While our current focus is on building and enhancing our Medicare services, it's important to note that we can sell life insurance and annuities. However, our commitment now is to become specialists in the field of Medicare, ensuring our clients receive the highest level of expertise and support in this area.

What plans will you offer my clients?

We believe in providing our clients with a comprehensive understanding of their insurance options. As such, we are more than willing to present supplemental insurance, Medigap, and Medicare Advantage plans to our clients.

Medigap is a policy sold by private companies to help cover some healthcare costs that Medicare doesn't cover, like copayments, coinsurance, and deductibles. It can provide additional peace of mind for clients who anticipate needing regular medical care or prefer predictable healthcare costs.

On the other hand, Medicare Advantage, also known as Medicare Part C, is an all-in-one alternative to Original Medicare. These bundled plans include Part A (Hospital Insurance) and Part B (Medical Insurance), and usually Part D (prescription drug coverage). Some plans may offer extra benefits like vision, hearing, or dental coverage. Medicare Advantage plans can be cost-effective for relatively healthy clients or those seeking more comprehensive coverage.

Each type of plan has advantages and can cater to different client needs depending on their health status, financial situation, and personal preferences. Our role is to help clients understand these options and guide them toward the best choice for their circumstances.

How do you protect my business?

Partnering with our firm offers a unique advantage in safeguarding your business interests. We understand the value of client relationships and are committed to protecting them. When you refer clients to us, we focus solely on providing the specific service needed without cross-marketing other products or services to these clients. This ensures that the integrity of your client relationship is maintained and your business is not at risk of dilution.

In today's competitive environment, there's a real risk of clients being pitched by other agents offering similar services. This could lead to confusion, dissatisfaction, and, ultimately, loss of business. However, when you partner with us, we help mitigate this risk. We provide superior service with our expertise, enhancing client satisfaction and loyalty to your business.

Maintaining control over client relationships is crucial in the financial services industry. We respect this aspect of business and collaborate with you, keeping you informed of all client interactions. Our goal is to supplement your services, not overshadow them. We aim to add value to your business through our partnership, enhance client satisfaction, and contribute to your ongoing success.

Detail your system for tracking referrals.

We understand the importance of accurately and transparently tracking referrals, so we've implemented a robust referral-tracking system. When you refer clients to us, we log all details into this system, including the client's name, contact information, the service they're seeking, and the name of the referring partner.

Our tracking system allows us to monitor the progress of each referral closely. We can provide status updates on our services to your referred clients and ensure that you're kept in the loop throughout the process.

Will you cross-market my clients?

We want to assure you that cross-marketing is against our policy. When you refer clients to us, we strictly adhere to providing only the services requested and needed by the client. We value the trust you place in us and respect the relationship you have with your clients.

Our commitment is to enhance your business, not compete with it. Therefore, you can rest assured that your clients will receive the specific assistance they need without being marketed additional services from us. This approach helps maintain the integrity of your client relationships and ensures a seamless service experience.

Discuss how this partnership can lead to mutual growth and benefits.

Our partnership presents an excellent opportunity for mutual growth and shared benefits. By collaborating, we can leverage each other's strengths, expand our service offerings, and provide our clients with more comprehensive solutions.

Your referrals are precious to us. They represent expanding our client base and are a testament to your trust in our services. We understand the importance of maintaining this trust and pledge to treat each of your referred clients with the utmost respect and professionalism.

We view each referral as an opportunity to demonstrate our commitment to excellence in service. We will work diligently to ensure your clients receive top-tier service, reinforcing their decision to trust you as their advisor. Treating your referrals with care will enhance your reputation and client relationship, increasing client satisfaction and loyalty. This, in turn, can lead to more business opportunities and growth for both parties, creating a fruitful and beneficial partnership.

What is your promise?

Our commitment to maintaining trust and prioritizing the client's needs is unwavering. We understand that the client's best interest must always be at the forefront of every interaction. We build relationships based on trust, respect, and mutual benefit.

If a referred client inquires about income streams or social security benefits, our policy advises them to reach out to you, their adviser. As experts in your field, you are best equipped to provide counsel on these matters. We respect the boundaries of our service provision and recognize the importance of your role in the client's financial planning.

In such instances, we will also inform you about the inquiry. This way, you can anticipate the client's questions and prepare for the discussion. This transparency ensures that we work together seamlessly, keeping the client's satisfaction and best interests as our shared priority.

ABOUT THE AUTHOR

In 1986, Al Kushner began the business of helping people understand Medicare in simple, plain terms that everyone can understand. His agency assigns expert sales agents to handle client referrals with their Medicare concerns.

Kushner is a best-selling author and Medicare insurance expert who has helped thousands of clients throughout his decades-long career. He is a warm and gifted communicator who has a passion for helping hard working seniors keep more of what they have worked a lifetime to save. Al speaks to audiences across the United States on the importance of Medicare and Social Security. To contact visit online at www.RealEasyMedicare.com or contact Al directly: Info@RealEasyMedicare.com or call 888-810-9725

Dear Reader,

Thank you for reading 10 Medicare Mistakes Financial Advisors Make and How to Avoid Them. We hope you found the book informative and helpful in navigating the complex world of Medicare.

As an author, I always seek to improve my writing and ensure that my readers are satisfied with my content. With that in mind, I kindly request that you take a few moments to leave a review of the book on your preferred platform, whether it be Amazon (http://www.amazon.com/dp/1632273322) , Goodreads, or elsewhere.

Your feedback is invaluable in helping me understand what worked well and what could be improved in future editions. It also supports other readers in deciding whether this book is the right fit for them.

Again, thank you for reading 10 Medicare Mistakes Financial Advisors Make and How to Avoid Them and for considering leaving a review.

Sincerely,

Al Kushner

www.ingramcontent.com/pod-product-compliance
Lightning Source LLC
Chambersburg PA
CBHW040757220326
41597CB00029BB/4977